Voices From A Silk-Cotton Tree

Acknowledgements
Thanks are due to the editors of the following: Penguin,
First Draft and *Draft 2* (Albert Poets), *Making Connections*
(Stride)

Previous publications
Lure of The Castadura (Bogle L'Ouverture 1989)
Behind The Carnival (Smith/Doorstop 1994)
The Sun Rises In The North (a collection of four poets)
(Smith/Doorstop 1991)
His work has also been widely anthologised.

As a visual artist John Lyons has exhibited internationally,
and his works are in public and private collections in the
UK, USA, France and Holland.

He is Director of the Hourglass Studio Gallery in Hebden
Bridge.

Voices From A Silk-Cotton Tree

John Lyons

Smith/Doorstop Books

for Jean Rees

Published 2002 by
Smith/Doorstop Books
The Poetry Business
The Studio
Byram Arcade
Westgate
Huddersfield HD1 1ND

ISBN 1-902382-41-2

British Library Cataloguing-in-Publication Data. A catalogue
record for this book is available from the British Library.

Typeset at The Poetry Business
Printed by Peepal Tree Press, Leeds
Cover picture by John Lyons

The Poetry Business gratefully acknowledges the help of Kirklees
Metropolitan Council and Yorkshire Arts.

CONTENTS

Hauntings

When flesh was their home
they were driven by a nameless energy
into fields and forests of literature,
blind to the pitfalls of words.

They hoped
glimpses of poets' lives
embalmed in their verse
would inspire their own;
but the searching *was* their poetry.

They are at odds now with the tangible.
Their presence is the chill in sun-lit places.
Their knowledge is beyond the reach of metaphor.
They have no words but their hauntings,
darkening silkcotton and sandbox.

Weather Vane

1

Not easy to understand
the hard fettle of Hughes' poetry
distilled from the Calder Valley,
where the sun keeps its distance
and the sky is a puckered tissue
greying everything.

Sometimes there is a blessing
in perceiving language in landscape:
Autumn in mid-Winter
with gamboge yellow, Indian red;
blue wood smoke lifting
amid scraggy sycamores,
their dark bloom of rooks' nests.

2

Quick as thought
I find myself in a Walcott haunt,
Trinidad, where miles of coconut palms
crowd the beach towards Chacachacare
like Columbus's first Arawaks at Punta Arenal.

His poetry is the sea.
Stanzas break into patterns of spume on sand,
endings enjambed, their meaning historic,
at one with the rhythm of the island.

Here the sun is gratuitous
and there is no escaping its indifference.
Here his metaphors are thin disguises
for the island's life-lust.

Back in the Calder Valley
I see the seasons falter,
forsythia deceived into bloom,
search for the dactyl in Caribbean *cassia*.

The Adoption

1

They tossed you three times over her.
She lay plugged with cotton wool,
cushioned in pale mauve satin,
lilies cold white on her embroidered breasts.

Afterwards, I looked at your blank face
and knew you were elsewhere with your pain.

Last night, through the rattle of rain,
it was not an owl I heard;
yes, live your tears and let me be
your mother now.

2

In the translucent gloom
he lay on his back under her canvas cot,
feeling her body's heat.
He tried to match his breathing to hers.
He dared not touch, hands skimming
where canvas bulged.

In that close space
he shifted for comfort,
felt her soft shape against his knee.

3

'Stop the giggling!
Don't excite yourself.
Besides, you are old enough now
to put your own clothes on.
And I must tell you,
I was the sister your mother never had.

Green Lust

Prologue

This forest-lust
was never mentioned
in old people's dem-say;
they would slip into silence,
screening knowledge
with coded body-talk.

When snoring disturbed
the shuttered midday,
and salipenta stalked chickens
in the dusty yard,
I dared the silence of the forest,
its thorned tongue,
its sap-green throat.

'Woo-too-too,'
warned the king-of-the-woods
from his perch in a pink poui.
With a sudden wing flap,
it spirited into the twilight
of the undergrowth.

It knew this forest's hauntings,
its secret histories, long before
it broke out of its shell.
'Woo-too-too!'
'Woo-too-too!'

But too-tool-bay with the lure of bush,
I was sucked into its green digestion,

into the interior night of the forest.
There was no sound but the muffled
fluttering of a frightened dove
inside me.

Epilogue

Later, I found myself
under the arc lamp of midday
lying on the beaten, burning yard
among the remains of a lizard's feast.

Farda

Meh farda was a man
who save his wuds,
his shakin larf fuh Christmas
and weddin parties
wen shots of vat 19,
sweetened with prunes,
put commas, never full stops
in stories he share wid meh uncles;
an after every chaser,
larf buss out,
larf buss out.

Every Sunday
meh fada was a fo-day mornin poitique
in Port-of-Spain market.
He pay fuh his cress an crab
wid patois and ole-tork;
an fuh langniappe,
he lef wid annoder bunch ah cress;
he lef de vendor, tut-tuts shakin wid she larf.

'Ah Lyons, yuh really hav a sweet mout,
yuh really have a sweet, sweet mout.'

Every day fuh years an years
meh farda ride he bike, Josephine,
to mek shoes in de city,
to stanup by he counter
shapin shoe leather
fuh farmers wid yam foot.
An doh ah didn't know it at de time,
de veins in he legs
was knitting varicose knots
fuh future pain.
Wen dey did topple im into bed,
'is obeah, is obeah,' de people said.

Father's Unmarked Grave

Ever since that jumbie bird
with stagnant-pool eyes bustled in,
stirred up the settled dust,
Father, I dream of you:

I dig the darkness
under a silk-cotton tree,
disturb your bones
which the earth claimed with ochre;
and I feel the yearning-for-a-hug love,
a stubble-against-toddler's-cheek love.
I search the weather map of your face,
see dark clouds gathering.

The day Mother died
you hid behind bedroom door
confiding to the gloom.
But I heard
your belly-sound of grief,
felt tears inside me,
lost my firm ground.

Carnival Shadows

Jour Ouvert.
A dull silver day.
Air so tight,
it ready to snap
into carnival madness,
into olemas.

Shadows, the mind's unspeakable
imaginings, strain
against the veil.
Soon pan syncopation
and the breakaway.
Death in dusty alpagats,
is possessed by his mask.
He stalks in the streets.
But the rhythm of life
he tries to suppress
with this stealth,
betrays him,
exposes his face.
He *wines* like the living
and doesn't give a damn.

Carnival Snapshot

Dawn came, silver-plated the night
into fo-day morning tense with carnival.

Jour ouvert, and a ragamuffin olemas was out early,
barely hidden behind home-made grotesquerie
and a falsetto voice:

'Madam, yuh want yuh yard sweepin
ah does sweep clean clean, yuh know.'

He began to *wine,* sweeping the air
with coki-yea broom in one hand,
a jingling cloth purse in the other.

Ma Magot, arms akimbo,
stood square at her front gate,
restraining a smile with fierce eyes
and crumpled forehead:

'Ah know yuh,
ah know is you, meh little scamp.
yuh cahn fool me. Ah know yuh
by yuh maga legs.'

'I ask yuh to clean-up this yard
two days ago. Go play yuh mas,
buh ah tellin yuh, yuh better be back
here by twelve o'clock, or is licks
in yuh backside from yuh fada,
yuh hear meh.'

La Jabless

(Trinidad folklore)

Why the silence now?
Where are those words
that led me to this secluded path?

Odd now the black clouds,
the peek-a-booing full moon.

There is no sound
of your breathing, your footsteps.

This is no dream:
Your perfume, like night lily,
still cloy, your laughter
still bell-like in my ear,
louder than the guaracha
in the Las Cuevas fete.

What is that white beast
passing through a shaft of moonlight?

I was found next morning
clinging to life,
the mark of a cow's hoof
blue-black on my face.

Soucouyant On Bonfire Night

Wen bangers,
rockets and pungent air
keep sleep away,
jus stare-up in de sky,
an yuh go barely see
a comet flyin low,
is Soucouyant, ah tellin yuh,
camouflage in bonfire glow.

Soucouyant!
Soucouyant!
Wey yuh dey?
Ah know yuh hidin
in de fire
an yuh not burnin.

Soucouyant find comfort
in dis explodin night,
an wid no caution,
fling sheself in flight
wid she vampire attire
a red an orange
ball-a-fire.

Soucouyant!
Soucouyant!
Wey yuh dey?
Ah know yuh hidin
in de fire
an yuh not burnin.

Watch out!
Watch out!

Soucouyant want to kiss yuh
wid she hot hot mout,
mark yuh wid desire,
leave yuh on fire.

Soucouyant!
Soucouyant!
Wey yuh dey?
Ah know yuh hidin
in de fire
an yuh not burnin.

The Douens

(Folklore spirits of children who die before being baptised)

Conceived in myth
we give them the substance of mind.
They are as real as the body's responses.

We give them feet turned backwards,
dada hair under straw hat
like a jumbie parasol.
We neuter their gender,
give them a face without features
but for a small round mouth-hole
for eating the mythical crab
and young sweet corn.

Mothers, christen your babies at birth!
Do not call their names in green open spaces.
Beware of river banks and forest glens;
they entice away your children,
these prankish Douens.

The Game-Keeper

Wild god of the *bois,*
the satyr's clone.
Who calls you Papa?
The agouti, manicou,
lapp and quenk.

You stalk hunters
in the green dusk
beneath balata trees,
mahogany and cedar.
The macaw's screech
is your fanfare:
you materialise
clothed with the forest
and the odour of animals.

We don't know
who you really are;
but you are real enough
to the killer hunter,
his last words muffled,
his weight on a strangling vine.

Everywhere A Workplace

Sometimes obeahwomen sit in airports
wearing several hats of different colours.
They carry a large bag of tricks,
mutter and chuckle to themselves.
The secret joke is never on them.

Lougaroo's Survival

Time for feasting, a desperate love
for survival: his gentle puncturing kiss,
like a lover's.

He conspires with a ripe moon
to conjure up the world of folklore.

Before the moon hides
in dark-grey folds of clouds,
the ritual, 'lougarooooooooooooooo.'

There is a turbulence of flesh:
a shaping of jaw, lengthening of canines,
knees crooking back, feet become paws,
armed with talons.

His air-nuzzling savours heifers.
In pastures they topple their bulk,
offer pale, stretched bellies.

Moco Jumbie

His knees scrape the crown of immortelles.
His eyes, level with the moon's cold face,
freeze clouds; his breathing
is a hurricane being born.

Stay clear of those strangling legs
astride the snaking country road
glittering like a cascabel in moonlight.

Take a different direction.
Dissolve into the silhouette of trees
abstract as myth against a canvas of moon colour.

Beware the poems you read.

Auguring With Wild Laughter

In grazing ground
circumscribed by a short tether
an old ewe staggered,
legs bitten to bone.

Just out of straining nuzzle-reach
a lamb lay, eye a snap-shot of terror,
throat a mess of flesh;
and on the trampled green, blood darkening.

Face impassive, fleece
lanolin-matted, stained red,
the ewe bleated and bleated.

The smell of slaughter
hung like a curse.

That night the village obeahman
shot at something moving like the wind,
heard a diminuendo of wild laughter.

Fauna's Warden

Prologue

Hunters, say 'bon jour, vieux Papa,'
say 'bon martin, Maître Bois.'
to that hairy old man tanned like hide,
leaves growing out of his beard.
Look away from his cloven hoofs.
He is the irascible keeper of forests.
He takes exception to the joy of slaughter.

I am omnipresent with my senses
in this green profusion.
Here distress is an odour more pungent
than fear: some quenk or deer cornered
by hounds, driven, not by sport,
but an instinct for the drug of blood;

and the animals' petrified silence
is the loudest cry, deafening.
The blaze in my eyes is the rage of forests;
and every tree and hanging vine
becomes the hunters' enemy.

Epilogue

An obeahwoman, gathering herbs
for fever, heard wind chimes:
bleached bones high in a silk-cotton tree.
and at its roots, guns, their killing efficiency
choked with rust.
'Bon jour, Maitre Bois,' she said, sniffing the air.

Not Every Old Woman Is A Soucouyant

That rheum-eyed woman
with rough-dry skin
tottering on the pain of arthritis
is butt for ragamuffins playing
away from their mothers' licking strap
and stinging tongue.

Over their doors, the horseshoe;
rice heaped a spell on doorsteps;
noughts and crosses in white chalk
construct magic barriers.

But that old woman has a doting grandchild
who calls her Mamie.
Sea moss, cooked to a jelly,
swivelled in hot milk and sugar
is her favourite drink;
not blood.

Ancestors Say Goodbye

1

The boat's 'booooooom'
in the bay bounced off mountains,
joined ancestral voices:

Dey leavin,
dey leavin de bush,
dove siesta lullabys.

Dey leavin sweet potato
to rootin pigs,
yams to run wild.

Dey leavin ajoupas
in cool valleys,
shacks clinging to hills
above seaside fishin towns.

Dey leavin de city bazodee
wid chantin poitique,
wid rumblin an dust.

Wey yuh goin?
Wey yuh goin?
Came de ancestral voices
like wind through
poui and poinciana.

Wey yuh goin?
Wey yuh rushin to?
Buh dey dohn look at de lan;
they leavin wid ruction
in dey head.

Lan weepin,
crapaud in de house
in de dark under bed;
cat gorn,
dog stray.

Buh wey yuh goin?
Wey yuh goin leavin happy rain,
days wash clean,
days wash wid sun?

Wey yuh goin
after all dem years
groin up wid breadfruit
and roast salfish?
I tellin yuh, yuh go miss
yuh limin,
yuh bacchanal.

2

Wind, like it malkadie,
rush across the Atlantic,
pushin water into hills, shiftin
shiftin into moving gullies.
Wind wild, wild
wid more power
dan de obeahman.

De Empire Windrush
like it too-tool-bay,
lurchin like a jack mule on de ocean,
sailin one side of de slave trade triangle.
Wind loud loud like it vex;
buh dis time, no dead cargo
to feed hungry sharks.

Dis time dey on dey feet
dancin on deck,
singin sex rhythms,
bush rum visions in dey head.

'No more catchin we nennen.' dey say.
Opportunity,
opportunity
in de mudder country.

Passage Home

As meh name is Mabel, I know wen dat black bird fly in
meh kitchen, I had to ban meh belly. I so full-up wid meh
daughter, Florette, is like a pregnancy in me head. Den de
letters begin to come from dat cole place. Englan no
mudder at all; not a country, milk dry up in she tut-tuts.

Englan is Florette cross to bear. Four letters in one week.
She didn't write home bout missin de cool fo-day mornin in
de Lavantie hills. She didn't write home bout missin de eart
smell after midday dongpour. She didn't write home bout
longing fuh roti an curry-goat. No, she write home bout
how people looks could kill she.

I could feel de sufferin
de way she 'l's crooked,
not correct on de line
like in children copy book.
She need meh!
She need meh!
Come hell or high water
I go have to go to Englan.

The Atlantic flexes
its sinews of water
dark with an unbearable history.
Mabel's guts heave:
a sensation more than nau-
sea. She sees grey shadows
braving the turbulence
in the ship's wake,
waiting   waiting.
Then the dumping

of spoilt goods;
a frenzied feasting:
flesh roukou red
against glistening ebony.
Screams skim the waters.

Silence.

The Ocean digests.
The Ocean conceals.

Where are the tomes
weighted
with the agony
of this history?

But how Florette tin so! Is dis meh one-an-only gurlchile
lookin as if she have marasma? Is dis de gurl who dem jamet
limin on street corners use to call bam-se-lambe? Wey it
gorn, de sparkle in she yeye? Eh-eh, ah never woulda believe
dis if ah didn' see it wid meh own two yeye. If she farda
come back now from de grave he gosay, 'didn' ah tell yuh
time an time again, who doh hear go feel. Yuh cahn say ah
didn' warn yuh. De only place fuh a gurlchile is home
lookin after she mudder an farda, not gallivantin to some
place behine Gord back.

Doh worry, meh gurl,
yuh mudder here now,
yuh mudder here now.

Under voices
without sun-polish,
piles of eddoes, yams,

ocroes, earth-textured echoes
of Port-of-Spain market.
They are tired, tired ground provisions.
They too crossed the Atlantic.

She couldn't find
soft candle and bay rum
to mix with nutmeg
for Florette's ague,
no zebapique,
no zebafam
for her menstrual pains;
no soursop bush for flu,
no shandilay for fever;

Crapaud is no dark angel
hoppin into drawing room;
black bird in England
is no jumbie bird;
they have no secrets to tell,
Mabel has no signs to read.

Am here nine months now,
Florette, meh gurl,
ah have a tie-up kerchief,
in meh bloomers
wid we passage back home,
there is a house waitin fuh yuh
in Sangre Grande.
We cahn stay here,
we cahn stay here
Lehwe go, chile;
lehwe go back to Trinidad.

The Drunkards

Cacapool rum toughened their throats,
left their minds like conch shells
echoing a sober past.

We judge their efforts to regain balance
as the grammar from which they make
sentences of their world.

All praise, all praise
to gravity and the certainty
of earth that checks their fall.

Livin In Bonne Langue

Look how he limin,
rhymin life wid language:

Coonoomoonoo
soften vexation wid music.

For seduction,
punkaloonks and doodoo
slip off de smoodness
of he tongue.

Even cut-eye and cheups
cahn stop he;
he mamaguyin:
'Hey meh cocotte,
how yuh lookin good so!
Eh-eh, look at de bamsie,
like it movin to sweet pan.'

An wen he cahn stan chupidness
from a chupidie,
he always sen im to Cayacou
an he givin serious fatigue:
'Like yuh went to school in August
an yuh bess subject is recess.'

Sometimes,
he farse-an-outa-place:
He yeye maco,
he tongue maco,
an everybody know
everybody business.
He faster dan bush telegraph.

An wen he have more guts

dan a calabash, he *bravé danchez*
walkin in de middle of city traffic, sayin:
'Bounce meh nah!
  Bounce meh nah!'

He love to dress-up
in he gabadene suit
an dowse heself in Old Spice,
an wen he see a mopsy,
put on a sagaboy swaga-walk.

He love a spree
like hog love mud.
He keeps firing shots of rum,
buh de only ting he killin
is he speech. It slurring
like an old gramaphone
runnin outa speed. Peppery souse
an cole water on he face fix im up
an he ready to leggo in a calypso:

From de waist up
he steady as a pillatree;
from de waist dong
he winin, wen ah tell yuh,
he winin, he really winin
an he shoutin:

'Bacchanal! Bacchanal!
Ah want to wine,
Ah want to wine on sometin.'

A oleman wid a droopy felt hat,
baggy trousers, a leghorn cock
under one arm, a bottle of sweet oil
in he han, shake he head and say:
'once a Trini, always a Trini.'

Where Strolling Is Prohibited

(For J.R.)

Not a place to go strolling in Trinidad;
especially when the sun is about to drop
out of sight, turn La Brea as black as its pitch,
make candle flies visible.

The beach, 'jus dong de road'
is two walking miles away,
but not in the flight pattern of crows.
That other predator, the mosquito,
with a longing for new, holiday blood,
does not warn with a 'fee-fi-fo-fum'.
They sing for joy in minute falsettos,
then in sudden silence, drill through
your unction of repellent.

Moths

Sleep-time in Down Town Port-of-Spain.
Between half-closed jalousies,
the voyeur's slit, they passed
in and out of street lamps'
ring of yellow light.

They were the species with lipstick
the colour of clotted blood,
and a second skin of satin.

Well before the tarnished pewter dawn
they vanished; then road sweepers came
with relentless bristle brushes,
tin-scoops cleaning up
more than the droppings of coconut vendor's donkeys.

'Like dem jamets was busy lastnite,'
a road sweeper said.

Trini Wisdom

In the evening shadows
of Toco's wild bush,
where the quenk and gouti run,
a wake stirs the trees
and the macaque adds
its descant screeches to the dirge.

Someone is left
to gather a shattered life
in this vigour of flora,
this dance of fauna;
and Trinis continue
wining their bodies
to soca and parang,
to maco-talk
and mauvais langue.

A Room In The City 1938

We lived on Queen Street
near the market-heart of Port-of-Spain
with its odours of over-ripe fruit,
ground provisions, open street gutters.

We squeezed and bumped around
in an apartment partitioned
by my father into a cobbler's workshop.

The only window faced onto the street.
It was shuttered against the maco's eyes.
Daylight made a stealthy entrance;
and what you couldn't see in the gloom
was best left alone. Murmurings in dark corners
were an introduction to jumbie stories,
soucouyant and La Jabless of later years.

My father was haunched
at his cobbler's bench, visions focused
with an Old Testament faith,
plying awl and waxed hemp, stitching soles
in the incandescence of a carbide lamp.

My mother mothered behind a folded screen
in a space not big enough to laugh in.
Life for me was lived in a four poster bed
with brass knobs, some small and perfectly
round for marble pitching.

Queen Street China

I gazed across
to China on Queen Street:
A tea shop, its one window curtained
with ducklings smoked and glazed soy-sauce brown;
a doorway through which disappeared
men stooped with an ancient history,
men with lean faces, the colour of jaundice,
betraying nothing.

They shuffled into a world
I could only fantasise about.
They had survived the crossing from Amoy to Trinidad
on the Riding Hood and the Dudbrook back in 1866.
Unhappy with indentured labour,
they were the deserters of sugar plantations,
the retrievers of a displaced culture
in a smoke-filled tea room.

The Diving Pond

Uncle Herbie's boys left Couva in Trinidad
to live in Rockley Vale, Tobago. They left a flat land
with murmuring bamboo grove,
mauby-coloured ponds which they dredged
for the mud-loving cascadoo.

In Tobago on grandmother's land
they could not scamper fifty yards on even ground,
nor stand the cloying intimacy of the bush.

They discovered a diving pond:
an ochreous soup with an odour of rich earth
and an archipelago of frog spawn.
This did not stop their diving.

The first grandmother knew of it
her blood pressure went up;
she rolled her eyes to the sky:

'Jehovah! Look at de cross meh have to bear,
an ole woman like me!'

They just stood there smiling, faces streaked
like delta tributaries, dry and cracked.

The Warning

1

'Crapaud smoke he pipe,'
Ma Joshua said,
'if he tink he could go
in dat jamet bed
widdout bringin dong
obeah on he head;
if he tink he could escape
mauvais-langue,
he better tink twice.
Ah tellin yuh, he spittin in de air
an it mus fall back on he.'

'Ah only tellin yuh dis
because he is yuh son
an ah know im
since he was in shut-tail
and couldn't wipe
de snot from he nose.'

2

'Dohn yuh cheups at meh, bwoi,
Ma Joshua dohn tell lie;
she like a granny to yuh.
Tek yuh han outa yuh pocket.
Yuh come inmeh house bole-face so
tellin me yuh courtin dat bacra jamet
livin only two doors away;
eh-eh, look at meh crosses.
Yuh jus outa short pants
an aready yuh tink yuh feelin yuhself
tinkin yuh is a big man.'

'A know dat red oman fass.
She muss be doin sometin
to mek yuh feel good.
Buh lemmeh tell yuh, sonny,
wat sweet in goat mout
sour in he bambam;
an besides, she got a sweet-man
livin in Lopino;
so watch yuh step.

Old Remedies

Something told me
it was more than a nose bleed,
put money in my hand,
gave me speed to run a mile
from Rockley Vale to Scarborough
to buy ice for her bleeding;
then back before Granma could say:
'Jack Robertson' (her favourite expression).

When I rushed into the house
I found her sitting on a wooden stool,
an enamel basin of blood between her feet;
around her head, a wrapped towel.
Auntie Abbot was soaking it
with last Christmas ginger beer
turned vinegar in the ashes
of the kitchen fireplace.

She looked up from her blood,
saw me enter, began to tell me
where to find coppers for ice.

'Here is the ice, Granma,
ah get it aready.'

That was the day I saw her eyes soften;
and until her death, she spoke
of her 'good granchile who fly like de win
to save meh life.'

The Builder

1

He observed men building houses:
how they cleared ground
for digging to bed-rock.

He watched them balancing,
with the body's knowledge,
pillatrees on steep slopes.

He marvelled at the way
things came together with intimacy
of halving joints, mortise and tenon,
constructing a logic men live by.

For a long time he stood beneath immortelles
in awe with corn birds weaving hanging nests;
he knew then it would take a life-time
of ingenuity to build the house
he wished to grow wise in.

2

It was hard work digging a pit of clay,
dancing in the straw with bare feet,
pugging mortar to shape rooms to his desire.

As he danced, he dreamed of moulding
a room around silence, a place in which to foetal-curl,
suspend thoughts of how to survive;
another, without corners,
walls smoothed to a mirror
with the friction of love.

He danced dreaming
of the one where he would store
the things he had given power to:
an owl's mummified wing,
his navel string, never planted,
withered like dead yam vine;
the cosmic pebble, like a bull's black eye
that almost struck his father down.

The last room was for his mother.
She died when he was nine.

Breakfast Shed and Pepper

1

Fo-day morning. City people
still hugged the fusty warmth of bedrooms,
deaf to the yard-cock's fanfare.
Stevedores refuelled on fried king fish, bakes
and greasy cocoa-tea in the Breakfast Shed,
a place of many kitchens a stone-pelt distance away
from big boats moored to Port-of-Spain quay.

These muscled, ebony men saw their mothers
through the steam of pots.
They knew that overnight king fish had revelled
with thyme, hot bonna pepper and shadow beni.
They knew that overnight the spirits of ancestors
had come to taste, to bless flavours of survival.

2

These days the Breakfast Shed draws
a motley crowd, like fowl to a feeding back-yard:
Retired civil servants, septuagenarians to a man
and buddies now, make a shit-talk-and-food *lime*,
give fatigue, *mauvais-langue* old bosses
who barred their way up the ladder.

Executives in the flush of business youth,
short sleeves and Trini-island pride,
tuck tie ends away from cow heel soup, cocoo and callaloo,
their maco-talk sharper than the pepper sauce
they spike their food with.

These days Europeans come, not to plant a flag.
Their lust is not for the search of Montezuma's gold,
but the Midas sun. The untanned enter slowly.

They linger over the speech rhythms of oral menus;
cooks are patient:
'... An above all, mine de peppersauce.' They say.

The well-tanned bee-line to their favourite kitchens,
order stewed king fish in Solomon-ah-gundy sauce
rice and peas, mauby or sorrel to put out fires
raging in their throats.

Pink Kimono

Never knew her name,
but can still see her standing
in the doorway of her small apartment,
a pink kimono like a cascade of silk
from narrow shoulders,
large wet eyes, a skin of pale yellow ochre,
and paler still where kimono fell away
from a small breast.

How like a delicate water-colour she looked,
hugging her wasp waist and holding back
an escaping smile.

Just before pitchoil lamps were lit
and coconut vendors put match to flambeau,
her sweet-men came: the sagaboys
with zoot suits and hats rakish over eyes.

From time to time, the bacchanal rhythm
with bottle-an-spoon. Everybody was a maco then:
complained about the ruction,
stared at her silks and gold bracelets.
'More in de motar besides de pestle,'
the neighbours say.

Navel String Of Poetry

1

I searched that misty place of memory,
found my navel-string tree of poetry:

I am back in blue-grey city dawns;
coconut vendors plying their trade
on street corners, odours of green coconut
freshly cut and the *piece monte* of donkey's dung,
green as wet season grass. The black tom
stalking pigeons on the roof
of the Chinese tea shop on Queen Street.
The market with its ceiling gothic
in wrought-iron and glass, its earthy smells
of home-grown crops and sweat of crowds jostling;
its echo of voices like rain on a galvanize house-top.
One block away, busses are rattling out of George Street depot,
pungent with exhaust fumes, engine oil and hot metal,
going East to Tunapuna, San Juan, Sangre Grande, Arima.

2

The Eastern Main Road is a deluge of traffic,
currents flowing in opposing directions.
Taxis pirate for trade with *bravé danchez* skill, and most days
a dead dog left swelling, ready to burst in the sun.
In this drama of speed and pollution,
the safest place is the gallery at the house-front.
Back-yard the mind senses metaphor, records
the noiseless riot of sweet broom, vervine and shandilay,
man-better-man, love vine and caccachat.
Here is where zandolies play and kiskadee
and sici-yea keep an eye on the bird-hunting cat.

3

Before words in syntax, the image,
like a chick breaking out of its egg.
Every pillatree holding up the house, every book margin,
every wall under threat: drawings made with
the charred remnants of the coalpot.
For colour, the spectrum of zennias,
chalk stones of yellow ochre, red-brown and grey
unearthed by the new-road tractor.
The scent of exposed earth
was *bois brande* to my libido:
drawings were rampant,
but not yet the budding of words.

4

Pleurisy, on the wings of the jumbie bird,
came, sat for seven days on my mother's forehead,
then took her away. I could not recognise
the cold mauve tint of her face, nor her stillness
among the living white lilies.

Years later on a dirt track in Tobago,
the feudal neighbour found me beating grief
into the ground, mouthing words only the earth understood.
She called a truce, spread the alarm across the cactus fence.

'Yuh callin yuh dead mudder spirit on me,'
my grandmother bawled.

Carnival Robber Talk

(In celebration of the Midnight Robber Mas)

Rastabarooba is my name.
I am offspring of Loupgaroo and Medusa.
At that tortured hour of my birth
impenetrable darkness enveloped the earth.
Fish from deep oceans nested in trees,
birds lost their feathers,
fledglings ate their mothers.

I am no Robber Mas-
querader. I am the reincarnated
of the deracinated:
Slaves of the Middle Passage
were my brothers and sisters.
I am the Leviathan
who broke the surface
of the blue-green Caribbean.

I am no Robber Mas-
querader. I am the rage of slaves
whose jettisoned bodies fattened barracuda.
I am empathiser with their humilation,
their pain, their ocean-muffled screams;
so heed the eloquence of my curse,
loosen the strings, empty your purse.

I am no Robber Mas-
querader. I am master of necromancy
the awesome changer of black history,
turning slave-hunter into the hunted
in rank, raw forests of Africa.
With the snap of my fingers

I can resurrect the African dead
from their Atlantic bed.

I am no Robber Mas-
querader. To carray like a crab for me
is certain disaster. I am wizard:
At the darkest hour of night
my powers are at their height.
These bones that hang rattling on my belt
was my last challenger who felt
the destructive force of my might.

I am no Robber Mas-
querader. I am your worst nightmare,
the canker twisting your mind,
your inner darkness, your fears,
the acid in your tears,
etching years of misery in your face,
I am your hopelessness, your apocalypse.

I am no Robber Mas-
querader. Don't tangle
with Rastarbarooba, re-maker of history,
the one who can dissolve your misery.
So empty your pockets, your weighty purses
or suffer the hellish power of my curses.
Rastabarooba! The reincarnated
of the deracinated.

The Lament Of Soucouyant

Do not chalk me barriers.
Your close-knit flesh
will one day too unravel
like a life-worn chemise,
beyond intercession,
beyond repair.

You too, one day will wish
to shed skin like a fer-de-lance,
and with fire-ball of thought,
take flight, desire for new blood
cramping your stomach.

You too will live the torture of calypso,
sensibilities jumping to the promise
of perpetual youth like a ghost tenant
in a body that can no longer *wine.*

Dream Recording

The iguana tongue
the giant crapaud ate
was catalyst to a mutation,
like my indigestion
with this dream
is inspiration for a poem;
my not knowing, like life,
what it means; words, words
in the swift wake of the pen;

till the sun brings
day into the room,
diverts this verbal stream
to another consciousness:
I see the mirror on the wall
reflect a sun-lit interior:
a man in a mask
the image of myself
scribbling away his life.

Bonfire

He stands before a licking, lickerish fire,
takes a shot of Old Oak rum.

'Fire one!
Fire one fuh love,
fuh redemption!'

There is no drumming,
no dancing;
only a fire bewitching the dark
with its glow, its crackle and hiss;
only a fire exorcising
this cold country's jumbies:
heinous histories,
like frozen ghosts
on the bonfire's tongue.

First Lesson

Beatrice, the Spanish mulatto
from Down The Main,
smelled of buttered toast.
Dresses slipped off her shoulders,
often got caught in the fat-folds
of her waist, her bamsie-crease.

Once, in the dusty gloom
of her apartment, she ripped off her chemise,
asked me to rub her back pain away
with rosemary-scented coconut oil.
She told me stories about the masseur
who became too-tool-bay about her,
this Spanish mulatto
from Down The Main.

Hauling In The Sein

With each rhythmic grunt
the fishermen haul you in.
Spilled out on moon-soaked sand
you are sea harvest now, bewilderment
fixed in your lidless eyes,
gills sucking emptiness.

Fishermen celebrate. They blow
syncopated harmonies on conches
calling the fish-tea cooks.

Like night gulls they come in a clamour,
brandishing tin-pans and calabashes.
Before the sun comes up
they shall be feasting on fish-tea.

Some green fig, onion, ah squeeze
ah lime, some thyme an a bonna pepper
drop in whole fuh flavour.
Is good fuh de brain.

Holyfield Scorpion

Through forest ceiling
patterned sky-blue and emerald green
sunlight, like the transfiguration,
struck a blue-black, zealous scorpion.

It was alert in its sheen
spoiling for a fight.
My foot hovered;

'By St Peter, by St. Paul,
by St. Peter, by St. Paul,' I chanted.

But in a blink the scorpion disappeared
into humus the same colour as itself.
I brought my foot down,
lived to write this poem.

The Tamboo Bamboo Ban

Before the hey day of Chagaramus
and American oil drums
hammered into music, tamboo bamboo
was the rhythm of Christmas and carnival.

It was tam tam tam and the bam bamboo.

I was only a shirt-tail toddler then,
put to bed at the first sign of dusk
shading the late afternoons,
when yard fowl crane its neck
with each gingerly stride, peering
into the coming night for the hen-house
and owls grow in confidence
with the darkening.

It was the time of the chantuelles,
leader queen of the carnival ban, singing:

'Who dead?'
and the ban answer:
'Canaan!'

'Who Canaan?'

'Canaan Barrow!'

And everybody sang the chorus:
'Canaan Barrow went to tong
an a red-army badjon lick im dong.'

And the ban pass
bouncing bamboo on the hard road:
boom-boom, boom boom,
boom-boom, boom boom.

Stick against bamboo:
tik-tik, tik tik,
tik-tik, tik tik.

Tamboo bamboo!

Mythomorphia

(The obeahman's drug)

He eats the eggs of jumbie birds
and his tongue vibrates in tremolos:
low register of the vowel 'o'.

His footfall is like the drift of feathers
on the substance of night.
No one sees him come,
knows suddenly he is there.

When day slips through
a fracture on the horizon,
his world is veiled with light
and he finds himself caged
in the constructions of storytellers.

Reading A Skull

1

In a place where winds howled in packs
savaging the scrub, I found a skull
yellowing in raw weather.
I wondered if the sheep had seen
its predator from those sockets,
and with tongue arched against ceiling of bone
had quivered a last, flat cry.

2

Often it comes
like a knuckle-hammer across the face,
rupturing a smile.

The pain goes beyond skin,
beyond muscle and bone,
pulps the heart,
fuses the circuit of nerves
in the pit of the stomach,
becomes an overture
to the opera of silence.

Storm

Emotions high
like corbeau near cirrus:
black specks wheeling
in an updraft of argument.

Sky a frown of clouds,
the wind, corrupted since Pentecost,
is into thuggery now:
a mentor to badjohns, molesters
baring the feathered arses of hens.

Yard cocks celebrate their spunk
braving necks in the squall.
They are euphoric with conflict,
flapping wings, cackling questions,
expecting no answers.

Then it comes like a fury:
thunder like heavy furniture crashing,
splitting sky. Dogs slink away
whimpering into their private comfort.
Cats snarl, spit hopelessly into the wind;
neighbours keep their distance
peering through jalousies.
'Jees-an-ages!'
'Jees-an-ages!

The First Labour Man

(For Tubal Uriah 'Buzz' Butler)

His was the tongue of polished silver
word-crafting in subversive argument
the people's penury, their frustrations.
He was a pikant in the flesh of government.

They said he was a man of science,
no obeahman of politics'
but custodian of ancestral secrets,
carrying into Council a weighty bible
and a fan as talisman.

The police said he was the danger-mind
behind the riots in the oil fields of Fyzabad
when pitch-oil was thrown on Charlie King
and a lighted match made flambeau of him.

With hard-wood batons and righteous force
the Police came; but the magic
of his disappearance was the people's gift;
and griots celebrate, embroidering
history into myth.

Mongoose

Sly mongoose, darg know yuh name.
Sly mongoose, darg know yuh name.
Mongoose tinkin he smart an bard
went into de midday fowl yard
lookin fuh fattest chicken,
dohn care if is rooster or hen
tief it to he secret eart den;
sly mongoose.

They came to Trinidad
wid dey artful dodgin an sneaky cunnin
as riot squads fuh snakes.
An after dey prune de population
of fer-de-lance an cascabel,
mapepire and macajuel,
dey get bored. Dey cahn beat pan
like de badjohns from Jon-Jon,
so dey start to lime like jamets
near people fowl yard an fowl run;
an in de heat of midday siesta
snake killers turn to chicken flesh fiesta.

Sly mongoose darg know yuh name.
Sly mongoose darg know yuh name.
Mongoose tinkin he smart an bard
went into de midday fowl yard
lookin fuh fattest chicken,
dohn care if is rooster or hen,
tief it to he secret eart den,
sly mongoose.

Gombo Gombo

In his sad rags he is a walking
talking universe of bugs, a safe house
away from killing soap.

He stands at an invisible lectern
in Woodford Square,
the people's university,
discoursing on politics.

His audience is a motley crowd,
more in awe at his eloquence
than the complexities of argument.

'Freedom of speech,' he was saying,
'is no respecter of class.'

Beyond Instinct

I believed the old sow knew.
She squealed assaults,
pulled on her rope,
four legs like stakes
driven at a slant
in the churned-up pen.

With her advantage in the mud
I kept falling in that tug-o-wills.

Cajoling produced an assertive grunt,
a snooty snout in the air
sniffing for deception.

A slap on the rump
brought rage to her eyes.
It was time to leap the fence
of her pen, save my skin.
Later, Farmer McKenzie
brought his boar to her.

Washing Away Red Ochre

Still tethered to you by my navel-string
we chased salipenta in the bush,
scrabbled for roots.

Later, nuzzling your breast
I heard the dark moon calling,
slipped into sleep.

Oh how you wept.
You painted my skin with red ochre,
laid me down,
scattered poui blossoms over me.

You entered a sacred place
made love to the first stranger,
empowered the moon.

It rose full pulling me awake
through a ruptured bleeding earth.

No One To Kiss It It Better

Your scrabbling in the guava scrub
for a life you lost too soon
scattered ground doves,
wings whistling to a blur.

The earth did not hug you.

The clouds, scrambled by your screams,
have long since melted away;
that patch of land wounded by your pain
has healed itself with meadow flowers.

You were left on your own
to spin dream-catcher stanzas
from folklore and old people's *côté ce côté la.*

Every morning you awoke
scanning dreams for your mother.

Black Band

His grief is in drought.
The sun has dried up his tears.

He seeks the cool, hugging dark
in the latrine under the hog plum.

Here, away from the uncompromising sun
casting shadows of truth, there is comfort

in not seeing clearly,
in not knowing.

Sling-Shot Boy

A humming bird limp
in the coffin of his palm.
It was a tiny gift of life to Nature.

It wrenched from the sling-shot boy
a love he did not recognise.
Remorse broke over him
like breakers in Bloody Bay.

'I must eat this bird
or feed it to the cat,' he said.

Bush Poetry

My school, the bush.
I was a brother of Emile.
Rousseau would have been proud.
I learned to read naturally, became
familiar with passages in my book
of forest, every leaf a word
in context with its subject:
mahogany, cedar, purple heart.

I listened to assonance:
The bamboo's words carried on Trade Winds.
Its strength of syntax is in its roots
holding together loose expressions:
the gulley-bank in awe
with its stream's turbulent rhetoric,
consonance of pebbles, tumbling.